SCHIRMER'S LIBRARY
OF MUSICAL CLASSICS

DOMENICO SCARLATTI

Sixty Sonatas

In Two Volumes

Edited in Chronological Order
from the Manuscript and Earliest Printed Sources
with a Preface
by
RALPH KIRKPATRICK

Volume I - Library Vol. 1774
Volume II - Library Vol. 1775

D1557910

G. SCHIRMER, Inc.

Distributed by

HAL LEONARD PUBLISHING CORPORATION
Winona, MN 55987   Milwaukee, WI 53213

Printed in the U. S. A.

The Sixty Sonatas have been recorded by
RALPH KIRKPATRICK
for Columbia Masterworks on L. P. S. L. 221

CONTENTS

VOLUME I

CONTENTS (*Continued*)

VOLUME II

FACSIMILES

TEXT REVISION

PREFACE

Domenico Scarlatti

Domenico Scarlatti was without question the most original keyboard composer of his century, but his true originality first became apparent only in later life. Born in Naples on October 26, 1685, he spent the first half of his life under the shadow of his more famous father, Alessandro Scarlatti, writing operas, cantatas, and church music, in a style that for the most part is an extremely competent but pale reflection of that of his father. Most of these works date from the years he spent in Rome, first as *maestro di cappella* (1708-14) to an ex-queen of Poland, Maria Casimira, and later as musical director at St. Peter's (1715-19). Little if any of his surviving keyboard music can be dated from this period. Even the reports of his brilliant harpsichord playing at this time date from many years later, and are probably colored in retrospect.

Only with his definitive departure from Italy in 1719, and after his father's death in 1725 does Domenico Scarlatti appear to have developed the style that has rendered him one of the greatest keyboard composers of all time. For nearly ten years he was attached to the Portuguese court as chapel-master, and also served as music-master to the young Princess Maria Barbara. Upon her marriage in 1729 to the heir to the Spanish throne, he moved to Spain, where he spent the rest of his life. Most of the five hundred and fifty-odd surviving harpsichord sonatas appear to have been written for this musically unusually gifted princess.

The earliest dated collection was published in 1738 under the title *Essercizi per Gravicembalo*, and dedicated to her father, the King of Portugal, by whom Scarlatti had just been knighted. From this time on (Scarlatti was now fifty-three) appears to date one of the most extraordinary stylistic developments of any composer's later years. Scarlatti hardly composed any more vocal music, but confined himself to the writing of several hundred harpsichord sonatas. In these he conferred on the binary form a variety and expressive range that have never been surpassed by any other composer. Most of these were collected at the end of his life in a series of volumes for the use of Maria Barbara, now Queen of Spain. All available evidence points to the astonishing fact that more than half of them were composed between the ages of sixty-seven and seventy-two, in a fever-heat of creative activity and in a constantly developing style.

Scarlatti died in Madrid on July 23, 1757, leaving behind him a few manuscript collections of sonatas that remained almost entirely unknown to the world at large until their partial publication by Czerny in 1839 and their virtually complete publication by Longo in 1906. Throughout the 18th century he was known largely only for his earliest sonatas, many of which were published in England. The general recognition that he first gained in England as a result of these publications was founded on the relatively limited scope of these earlier works. Dazzling as they are, they have served in their own time, and ever since, to give Scarlatti the reputation of a happy, capricious mannerist. It is only with the later sonatas that a total expressive range becomes apparent that runs the gamut of an entire fund of distilled life-experience.

The Present Edition

The sixty sonatas of this collection have been chosen to represent as directly as possible the expressive range of Scarlatti's harpsichord music and the evolution of his style. They also supplement my *Domenico Scarlatti* (Princeton University Press, 1953). To this book I refer the student and player of Scarlatti for the fullest yet available account of his life and background, for a detailed account of his keyboard music and the instruments for which it was written, for general recommendations concerning performance, for a copiously illustrated essay on Scarlatti's ornamentation, and for complete catalogues of the sonatas and their sources.

Scarlatti's stature as a composer has been obscured in all hitherto published editions not only by editorial interferences with his text, but by the indiscriminate mixing of early and late works, and by the ruthless separation of the many sonatas that were conceived in pairs.

The present edition is the first that presents Scarlatti sonatas in chronological order, and that respects their original pairwise arrangement. It is still not generally known that nearly four hundred of the five hundred and fifty-odd Scarlatti sonatas are arranged in pairs in the original sources. (A few even are arranged in triptychs.) As I can testify from experience, the balancing and complementing relationship of the sonatas arranged in pairs greatly aids the player in extracting the full scope of their expressive content. Although it is evident that the sonatas of a pair were sometimes played separately, just as Bach sometimes separated his preludes and fugues, most of the later Scarlatti sonatas are obviously intentionally coupled in pairs. The pairwise arrangement of sonatas in the present edition begins with Sonatas XV and XVI (the earliest sonatas are not so arranged), and continues throughout, with the exception of the single sonatas XXI, XXII, LIV, and the triptych comprising Sonatas XLIX-LI.

The present edition is drawn from the sources closest to Scarlatti (no autographs are known to exist), and contains no editorial additions whatever that are not identified in the text or accounted for in the text revision at the end of the second volume. I have tried to let nothing stand between Scarlatti's text and the performer. This seems especially desirable in view of the distorting and often misleading indications for performance with which most editions of Scarlatti are obscured.

By refraining in the text from indications for performance, I have hoped to encourage the player to use and to cultivate his musical imagination. I have great confidence in the imaginative capacities of any musically inclined person. The arbitrary dictates of editors and the slavish following of them by parrot-performers, both amateur and professional, are no more essential to the normal musical organism than are crutches to the art of walking. People who are not physically incapacitated, or unnaturally lazy, need not be given crutches; they need only to be told or shown how to walk. Many can learn for themselves, if they be but encouraged to make the attempt. Potential musical imagination is a faculty much less rarely bestowed than is commonly believed. It is part and parcel of any natural human interest in music.

PERFORMANCE

While volumes could be written about the sixty sonatas of the present collection, and their performance, my own specific ideas regarding their interpretation will illustrate themselves far better in my recorded performances (Columbia) than in any verbal explanation. My desire in the ensuing sections is not to indicate conceptions or methods of performance of any particular piece, but to share with the players of this edition, as with my pupils, a glimpse into my own working habits; to aid the player in formulating those general principles and methods of practicing and of sharpening the ear which not only form the basis of my own interpretations but are so fundamental that they might serve equally well as a basis for interpretations radically different from my own.

For me the working out of a musical interpretation or the solving of a technical problem is inseparable from the necessary life-long process of training the ear. No ear is so dull that it cannot be trained; no ear is so sensitive that it cannot be taught or teach itself to hear more; no emotional capacities or sensory perceptions are so complete that they cannot be further developed. In every piece of worthwhile music there is always something that can still be discovered, always something that will have escaped its most experienced and most sensitive performer. Any interpreter who is not a parrot-performer knows the experience of sudden revelation or of gradual new light on a piece he may have already played for many years. Yet many of these revelations and new understandings need not await the accident of circumstances or the passage of time. Often they can be brought about by a few provocative comparisons or by a few simple self-imposed questions. For much of what follows I have borrowed the religious techniques of catechism and examination of conscience. In the guise of the general questions and answers of a kind of catechism I have outlined certain guiding principles that I have already discussed in the chapter on performance of my *Domenico Scarlatti*. The remaining specific questions, for which the asker has himself to seek the answers, are those that I ask mys 'f or a pupil in the course of preparing an interpretation. Most of these questions are applicable, not merely to Scarlatti, but to all keyboard music. I seize the opportunity, however, of appending them to a set of texts that are ideally—and provocatively—untampered with.

These questions, and the simple and constant search for their answers, can do more to heighten musical sensibility and interpretative imagination, to assist in the orderly formation of the necessary techniques, than any other one set of influences. Often, once certain sensibilities and working habits are established, these questions need no longer be consciously or analytically posed. They answer themselves in an instinctive synthesis of the feeling and functioning musical organism. Above all, they are questions posed to the physical organism, to its preferences, capacities, and sensibilities—and not to the mind. The conscious approach implied by these questions has no value in itself. It is valuable only as a stimulus and a challenge to the instinctive sensibilities, as a means of sharpening them, of pitting them one against another, of assisting their natural ordering and interaction, of freeing them from the dead weight of inertia and of inhibiting habit.

As every composer and writer knows, there is no better way of finding out what one really feels than having to set it down on paper, or having to communicate it through an artificial and restricted medium. A composer cannot write down an orchestral score without having eliminated every element of the haphazard and non-organic; he has to do much more than merely float on the seas of his own emotions. He must adopt definite concrete means of conveying those emotions through a medium over which he no longer has any direct control, nor any control at all other than the manner in which he has set his notes down on paper.

The performer's problem is less formidable, but similar. He must be able to marshal the spontaneity of his sensations into a consistent, ordered performance which he can produce at any time and under any circumstances. To this end, he must sense what elements of a piece are fixed and unchangeable in their relationship to each other, what is basic syntax and structure, and what is mere rhetorical inflection, what can be improvised and altered from performance to performance. Only by this security in relation to basic musical elements can he achieve true freedom and spontaneity in performance. The ability to make departures depends on a thorough knowledge of what one is departing from.

FINGERING

Questions answered:

Is there a musical solution to every problem of fingering?

Yes, except when the hands really cannot reach wide intervals meant to be sounded simultaneously. Then, however, there is generally a less efficient but musically acceptable solution in the form of arpeggiation.

What is a good fingering?

One that involves an economy of motion and a consistency that ensure security, and that most simply and directly exposes the musical content.

What is a bad fingering?

One that introduces unnecessary motions and changes of hand position that hinder rather than assist the expression of musical content.

What is the cause of much stumbling and inaccuracy?

Undecided and inconsistent fingering, and poorly prepared shifts of hand position.

How can a problem of fingering be solved in passages where stumbling and inaccuracies occur?

By writing down and following an orderly and consistent fingering, and by later revising it, if necessary, for even greater convenience and musical suitability.

If I write down careful and consistent fingerings for at least three Scarlatti sonatas, and test them out and revise them so that they really work in execution, will I be able to finger the remaining sonatas satisfactorily?

Yes.

If I learn at least six Scarlatti sonatas with carefully written-out fingering, will I be able to dispense with writing out all but unusual passages in the others?

Yes.

Questions to ask:

What fingering permits the maximum legato grouping of notes without change of hand positions?

What fingering best permits the transition from one hand position to another?

Which intervals demand legato and which permit detachment?

In this chord passage, have I found the smoothest possible fingering? Can I cover an undesirable detachment in one voice by making a smooth progression in another? Have I eliminated unnecessary substitutions of finger, and have I satisfactorily coordinated those that are necessary?

In this passage in broken harmony, what fingering adapts itself with the greatest security to correspond with the underlying chord progression?

Is this phrase best expressed by a fingering permitting an unbroken legato, or by one that expresses the articulation of certain intervals by automatically detaching?

Is a quiet hand advantageous here, or is there a movement of the hand or a shift of hand position that will help to bring out the musical content of the phrase?

In these repeated notes, which grouping of changing fingers feels and sounds best? Is it a pattern of four, three, or two fingers? Is it a passage by any chance that sounds better without a change of finger?

Do certain notes sound better with releases that are as sharp and as accurately timed as their attacks?

Will this fast passage sound less eloquent, or more crisp and brilliant by means of an accurate timing of the releases as well as the attacks of its component notes?

Does a staccato or merely a simultaneous timing of the release of one note with the attack of the following note sound better here?

On certain notes is it better to make two separate impulses, one for attack and one for release, or to make only one impulse to embrace both attack and release?

Do certain notes sound better with a gradual than with a sudden release? Do they sound better when held and allowed to die away or to be covered by the attacks of succeeding notes?

Does a legato here enhance or obscure the rhythmic energy of this passage?

Will overlapping add to the effect of legato? Will it add harmonic richness to the inflection of dissonant passing tones, or will it diminish brilliance by rendering releases imprecise?

Do certain octave passages sound better when played with a floppy wrist, or with a firm wrist and an unbroken connection between forearm and hand?

Do certain passages in consecutive thirds or sixths sound better when played detached, with the same fingers, like octaves?

In passages outlining broken harmony, which sounds better: to play them melodically, or to sustain the harmonies with the fingers (or the pedal)? Is it desirable in some such passages to make shadings in the sustaining of underlying harmony, from non-sustained, through partly sustained, to fully sustained?

TECHNICAL PROBLEMS

Questions answered:

How can I learn to play accurately and securely a passage that causes me technical difficulties?

1. Break it down into its smallest elements.

2. Make sure of a hand position or a series of hand positions and their preparations and transitions that will most efficiently negotiate the passage. (By efficiency is meant the greatest economy of motion and the greatest ease with relation to extracting the specific musical content of the passage.)

3. Bearing in mind the position chosen as the best, negotiate the smallest elements, for example in a scale, arpeggio, or octave passage, two notes, first notes 1 and 2, then 2 and 3, etc., at a tempo and with deliberateness of preparation such as to ensure absolute security. Then practice groups of three and four notes in the same manner, up to the number of notes comprising a logical small division of the passage in question. Practice each group of notes at a tempo and with a preparation such that even before beginning the group you may be dead sure of its accuracy. It is by this predetermining of movements or groups of movements that an absolute accuracy can be ensured. (Inaccuracy is nearly always the result of a movement that has been inadequately or improperly prepared.) Especially at first, practicing of this kind demands the utmost concentration. Properly established habits of preparation and movement later become largely automatic.

4. After the accuracy of the separate small groups has been established beyond any doubt, the transitions between groups should be studied, first groups 1 and 2, 2 and 3, etc., then increasing numbers of groups, up to the limits of the next larger musical section, bearing in mind now, not only the preparation and the movement necessary to execute the separate small groups, but the preparation and movement necessary to negotiate two or more of these groups and the transitions between them. It is possible to solve any technical problem by separating its component materials into their respective units, and by determining the forces that connect them, in exactly the same manner that a mason can lay a wall of brick or stone with absolute sureness of determining its security by the proper laying of his foundations and the placing of his bricks and stones.

What is relaxed playing?

A balance of tensions and releases

What causes stiffness?

Maintenance of a continuous level of tension. All balanced movement is based on a curve of increasing or decreasing tension.

What most affects the character of any given note or passage?

Its preparation in advance. By the time the note or passage arrives it is often too late to control it.

Questions to ask:

Do I give myself signals that I can execute? Or am I like a bad conductor whose signals to his orchestra are too sudden and not immediately intelligible?

Is the cause of a mistake such as a wrong note or a false start to be found at the point of its occurrence, or is it to be found in a faulty preparation during the passage or silence preceding it?

Since I can play this passage perfectly by itself, where does the false movement or faulty preparation lie preceding it that causes me to stumble when I play it in the context of the piece?

Do I stumble in the repetition of this phrase when I always play it perfectly the first time because I have not grasped the physical difference in preparing it as a continuation or a renewal of movement rather than as a beginning?

Does the occasional failure of my hands to play exactly together arise from my manner of attacking the notes in question, or from my manner of preparing that attack?

ORNAMENTATION

Questions answered:

(For the fullest available information concerning Scarlatti's ornamentation, and for explanation of my terminology, see my *Domenico Scarlatti*, Appendix IV.)

Are ornaments played on the beat?

Yes, according to the most reliable 18th-century evidence.

Do the note values of Scarlatti's appoggiaturas indicate their length in execution?

Only rarely, and never consistently.

What do these signs mean: tr, and ∿ ?

Trills, according to the best available evidence, from above.

What is the meaning of the term *Tremulo*?

Apparently the same thing as a trill.

What does Scarlatti mean by the wavy line ∿ following a note?

That the note is to be prolonged beyond its written value.

Questions to ask:

Is this appoggiatura long or short?

Are there any clues in parallel passages as to the length of this appoggiatura?

Is this a short trill or a long trill?

Where does this trill stop?

Does this trill have an appoggiatura function?

Is this trill at constant speed, or does it begin slowly and speed up?

Does this trill require a termination, or did Scarlatti intend its omission?

Can this trill which is diatonically prepared from above conceivably be executed as a tied trill?

Is it desirable in this piece to add trills or appoggiaturas where they have not been indicated in the text?

PHRASING

Questions answered:

What is phrasing?

Phrasing is the uniting and organizing in performance of what belongs together, and the separation of what belongs apart. Furthermore it is the demonstration of the relationships of notes; it is the demonstration of the differences and gradations of activity and passivity, of tension and relaxation. It parallels the organization, balancing, and punctuation of gesture and of speech.

What is articulation?

Articulation, in the sense in which I use the word, is a subsidiary of phrasing. Articulation is the mere detaching or connecting of notes.

What are the best ways of marking phrasing and articulation?

For breaks, ⸵ or V ; for indivisible connections, square brackets, ⌐▢⌐ ; for partially connected divisions, broken square brackets, ⌐▢ ▢⌐ ; for small divisions embraced by a larger division, concentric square brackets, ⌐⌐▢⌐⌐ ; for detachment, dots, · , for emphasis, tenuto marks, — . Large phrases can be marked ⟋ at the beginnings and ⟍ at the ends, without obscuring the note picture with extended square brackets. Slurs, ⌒ , should only be used for what is actually to be played legato, for what vocally would embrace but a single syllable. Slurs embracing several syllables or several divisions of articulation are misleading.

How can I best understand the melodic contour of a phrase?
By singing it, or by singing its main outlines.

How can I best understand the rhythmic shape of a phrase.
By dancing it.

Questions to ask:

What are the largest musical divisions of this piece?

What are the next largest musical divisions, the next largest, and so on?

What are the smallest units of this piece?

What are the next smallest, and so on?

What notes form themselves into indivisible groups?

Where are the breaks between groups of notes?

Does this group of notes come to a full stop before the beginning of the next, or does the end of one group also form the beginning of the next?

Of several breaks between groups of notes, which are primary and which are secondary? For example, which correspond to periods, which to commas, which to breaks between words, between syllables?

What is the pattern of phrase lengths in this piece? How can the phrase lengths best be counted in terms of beats or measures?

Are these short fragments to be considered separately and independently, or do they merely contribute to the more important unity of a larger phrase which embraces them?

Are these short repeated phrases that are so common in Scarlatti to be played separately and given contrasting inflection, or is their inflection to be varied only so subtly as to make them appear but as units in a larger phrase which embraces them? For example, in a repeated two-measure phrase, do I count 1-2, 1-2; or 1-2-3-4? Similarly, in repeated four-measure phrases, do I count 1-2-3-4, 1-2-3-4; or 1-2-3-4-5-6-7-8?

Are certain triple repeated phrases to be played as AAA, ABA, or ABC? Are they independent, or part of a larger phrase?

MELODIC INFLECTION

Questions answered:

What is the measure of the significance of melodic intervals?

Vocal feeling.

Questions to ask:

What is the vocal feeling of these various intervals, either rising or falling?

What differences do I detect in the vocal feeling of conjunct and of disjunct melodic motion?

What is the vocal feeling of these changes of melodic direction?

To what essential notes can the melodic outline of this phrase be reduced? Which are fundamental notes, and which are decoration?

Does this line represent one vocal melody, or does it outline the melodic progressions of more than one voice?

Have I understood the sustaining power of rhetorical silence?

Have I achieved through the handling of the various degrees of legato, overlapping, juxtaposition, and staccato, some measure of the richness of the sung or spoken word, with its variety of attacks and interruptions of sound produced by the different consonants?

Questions answered:

What is essential to an accurate understanding of the melodic and harmonic expressive capacities of any piece?

The ability to sing any of its lines.

What is the first short-cut to the harmonic understanding of any piece?

The singing of its bass.

What is a sure guide to the harmonic nuances of any piece in their utmost detail?

The ability to sing any note of the piece in relation to any other.

How on a non-sustaining instrument do I bring out the active character of a tone that has ceased to sound?

By imagining the sustaining of that tone and playing the others in relation to it.

How can I best sustain in performance the subtleties of harmonic inflection of decorations and figurations?

By carrying on in the inner ear a kind of sustained thorough-bass accompaniment based on the fundamental harmony of the piece. Against this the subtleties of inflection of harmonic detail can be accurately and sensitively felt.

Questions to ask:

What is the harmonic basis of this piece in simple chordal harmony?

Have I been able to give as convincing a performance as possible of the whole piece in terms of its simplest chordal harmonies?

What chords are consonant, and what are dissonant?

When dissonances are present, are they essential to the fundamental harmony, or are they produced by suspensions or by melodic decorations?

What chords are active, in that they are pulling towards another chord?

What chords are passive, in that they give a feeling of repose, that they do not necessarily pull towards another chord?

What notes of this chord are dissonant with its bass?

What notes are consonant with the bass?

What notes of this chord are dissonant among themselves?

Of the notes of this chord, what is the relative degree of their activity (pull towards another note) and of their passivity (lack of inherent pull towards another note)?

Does this note which is common to two successive chords diminish or increase its activity in its successive context?

Of these two chords, which sounds more, and which less intense (active)?

Of the notes of this melodic figuration, which are consonant with the prevailing harmony? (In other words, which are chord tones?) Which are dissonant with it? (Which are non-chord tones?) What are the differences in their feeling? (If the sound of the prevailing chord has died away, might I not do well to strike it again against each note of the melodic configuration in order to hear its relationship accurately? Should I not be able, however, to hear it sustained accurately in my inner ear without having to strike it again?)

What key is this passage in? What is the feel of its component harmonies in relation to the tonic? Which is stronger (more active), which weaker (more passive)?

Is this passage modulating to a new temporary tonal center, or is it merely borrowing notes from other keys? What are the borrowed notes? How do they feel?

In this modulatory passage, which are the sensitive notes that announce the new key? Where is the new key definitely established?

Is this a final or a temporary cadence?

What is the difference in feeling between this chord in one key, and the same chord in another key? (For a very simple example, what is the difference in feeling between a C-major chord in C major, and one in G major?)

In what areas of this piece does the greatest harmonic and tonal tension reside?

What are the areas of this piece that are most remote from the home tonality? How do they feel in relation to the piece as a whole?

What are the areas of the piece in which harmonically and tonally something new is likely to be said, and those which confine themselves to confirming what has already been said?

TEMPO AND RHYTHM

Questions answered:

What is meter, as defined for our purposes?
A regular grouping of beats, or a regularly recurring rhythmic pattern.

How can one differentiate meter from rhythm?
Meter in our terminology is essentially regular, rhythm irregular. Rhythm is derived from the imposition of irregularity on regularity.

By what is a beat influenced?
By its preparation and by its subdivisions.

How does a downbeat achieve significance?
According to the nature of its preparation by an upbeat.

What parts of the pulse can best be used to maintain or alter a tempo?
The offbeat parts, for example beats 2 and 4 in 4/4; 2 and 3 in 3/4.

What is the expressive basis of rhythm?
Physical movement, whether pulse, breathing, verbal declamation, bodily movement, or a combination of these factors.

On what is all musical movement based?
On the relationship of impulse, activity, and repose.

In terms of rhythmic movement, which notes are most active?
Fast notes as contrasted with slow.

What in the physical organism produces this activity?
Motor impulses, which may give rise to one movement or to a group of movements.

What is the progression of movement in a series of notes or steps?
From impulse to activity to repose.

What notes represent the propulsion of a new impulse of movement?
Fast notes following slow.

In a change from slow to fast motion, what note or step sets off the new rate of speed?
The first fast note or step.

In a change from fast to even, slow motion, what note or step first establishes the slower rate of speed?
The second slow note or step.

What notes, when not otherwise qualified, form indivisible rhythmic groupings, or rhythmic syllables, to be negotiated on the momentum of a single impulse?
Active faster notes moving towards the repose of slower.

What creates rhythmic polyphony?
Different rates of speed in different voices, and non-simultaneous occurrence of accents and impulses.

What kills rhythmic polyphony in performance?
Simultaneous accents in all parts, subdivision of long notes which deprives them of their relative repose, excessive subordination of irregular movement of note values to the regular movement of the basic pulse.

How does one voice influence another rhythmically?
Partly by subdivisions of the beat, but largely by the enchainment of impulses from active upbeats.

On what is a convincing rubato based?
On notes that are active harmonically (dissonant) and rhythmically (off-beat or upbeat), and on breaks or turning points of melodic contour.

Does the activity of a piece always begin with the first note or chord?
No. Sometimes activity begins only with the first change of harmony, or with the first acceleration of motion.

How is an indestructible coherence achieved in a musical or a dance phrase?
By its incorporation into a continuous gesture rooted in an expansion or contraction of the diaphragm, corresponding to an inhalation, sustaining, or exhalation or breath.

Can this coherence be prolonged even over a long silence?
Yes.

Is it always possible, by incorporating them into the continuity of a larger gesture, to give detached notes a feeling of connection?

Yes.

Can the imaginary choreographing of Scarlatti sonatas be overdone?

No.

Questions to ask:

On what rate or rates of movement is the tempo of this piece based?

At what rate of speed do the fundamental harmonic progressions of this piece move? Is there change in the rate of these progressions? Where?

Does this passage move one to a bar, two, four, or three?

Does the tempo remain constant throughout the piece, or does it change or fluctuate?

What is the fastest tempo at which the melodic figuration and harmonic fluctuations can remain clear?

What is the slowest tempo at which the expression and the continuity of the piece can be sustained?

Is the pulse continuous throughout the piece, or is it broken? If the latter, where?

Is there more than one basic pulse in this piece? For example, does it sometimes move simultaneously in duple and triple pulse?

What note values of this piece imply an actual physical movement? Which can be stepped? Which pronounced by the tongue?

Are the fast note values expressive of actual movement at that rate of speed, or are they merely animations of an underlying slower rate of movement?

What is the bodily movement characteristic of this piece? How would you mime it?

What best expresses the quality of movement imagined in this passage, legato or staccato?

What are the significant points of change of rhythmic motion in this piece?

What are the indivisible rhythmic units of this melodic line?

Do these fast notes following a slower note represent a genuine new rhythmic impulse, or merely an animation of an underlying long note?

What is the simplest possible fundamental rhythmic outline of this phrase?

What is the enchainment of upbeats in this passage?

Are these syncopations really syncopations of the prevailing pulse, or are they the temporary imposition of a new pulse? Or do they represent an opposition to the regular pulse of an irregular rhythmic shape?

DYNAMICS

Questions to ask:

How many separately distinguishable colors does this piece seem to have?

Does it have one color throughout?

Could it be conceived in two simultaneous colors throughout?

Does it have sections of contrasting colors? If so, where do they lie?

Does it have possible gradations within an over-all unity of color or within separate sections?

Would this piece best be conceived in terms of solo, of tutti, or of solo and tutti?

If only two colors were available for this piece (solo and contrasting solo, or solo and tutti), how would they best be disposed?

If only three colors were available (solo, contrasting solo, and tutti), how would they best be disposed?

What orchestral effects, or imitations of non-keyboard instruments can I detect in this piece?

Will unity gain more than variety in the inflection of certain repeated phrases?

To what extent is the thickness and thinness of Scarlatti's keyboard writing indicative of the dynamic scheme of this piece?

Is the effect of a contrast in keyboard figuration or of a contrast between high and low registers enhanced or swallowed up by a corresponding change of dynamics?

EXPRESSIVE CHARACTER

Questions answered:

What is the basis of musical performance?

Demonstrating the similarity between what is like, the difference between what is unlike, and the gradations of values between what is more and what is less.

Can any of the foregoing musical divisions into which these questions have been organized be isolated in actual performance?

No. They can only be isolated in study and in practicing. Melody, harmony, and rhythm are constantly influencing and qualifying each other. This is why, within the limits of correct syntax and of inherent character, there are always several possible valid interpretations for any piece of music. No piece of music that has any life in it can be subjected to any one "definitive" interpretation. Its life is dependent on the conflict, cooperation, and constantly fluid equilibrium of its component forces.

Questions to ask:

Is unity or contrast more important to the expression of this piece?

Is this piece in one mood throughout?

Or are there several moods? Are they allied or sharply contrasted?

Is there a gradual evolution of mood?

Have I looked at this piece in such a way as to understand its inherent character, or have I rendered it the victim of my preconceptions?

Am I using these sonatas as vehicles for my instrument, or am I using my instrument to play these sonatas?

If I have been able to answer for myself the questions in the preceding pages, is it surprising that I need to ask very few questions concerning expressive character?

Sonata II (K. 7) in the *Essercizi*

Sonata VII (K. 44) in Venice XIV

Sonata XVII (K. 119) in Venice XV

Sonata XXII (K. 140) in Worgan

Closed,
symmetrical
2

Sixty Sonatas

Edited by Ralph Kirkpatrick

Domenico Scarlatti

K. 3
Essercizi 3, Venice XIV 31
Longo 378

42916×

4

K. 7
Essercizi 7
Longo 379

42916

42916

6

K. 16
Essercizi 16
Longo 397

60

65

70

75

80

85

90

95

101

107

K. 18
Essercizi 18
Longo 416

29

32

34

36

38

K. 28
Essercizi 28
Longo 373

58

64

70

76

82

88

K. 29
Essercizi 29
Longo 461

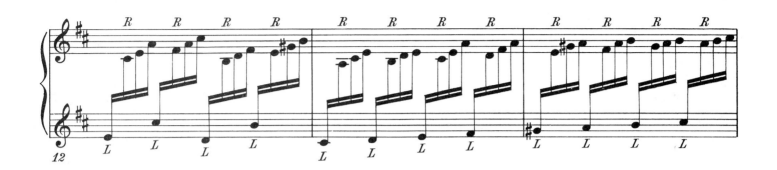

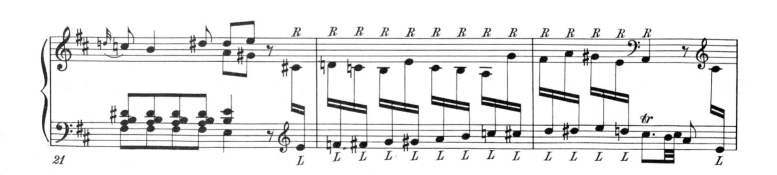

22

42916

24

42916

26

K. 44
Venice XIV 2, Parma II 20, Worgan 14
Longo 432

42916

28

83

89

95

101

107

(MORDENT)

113

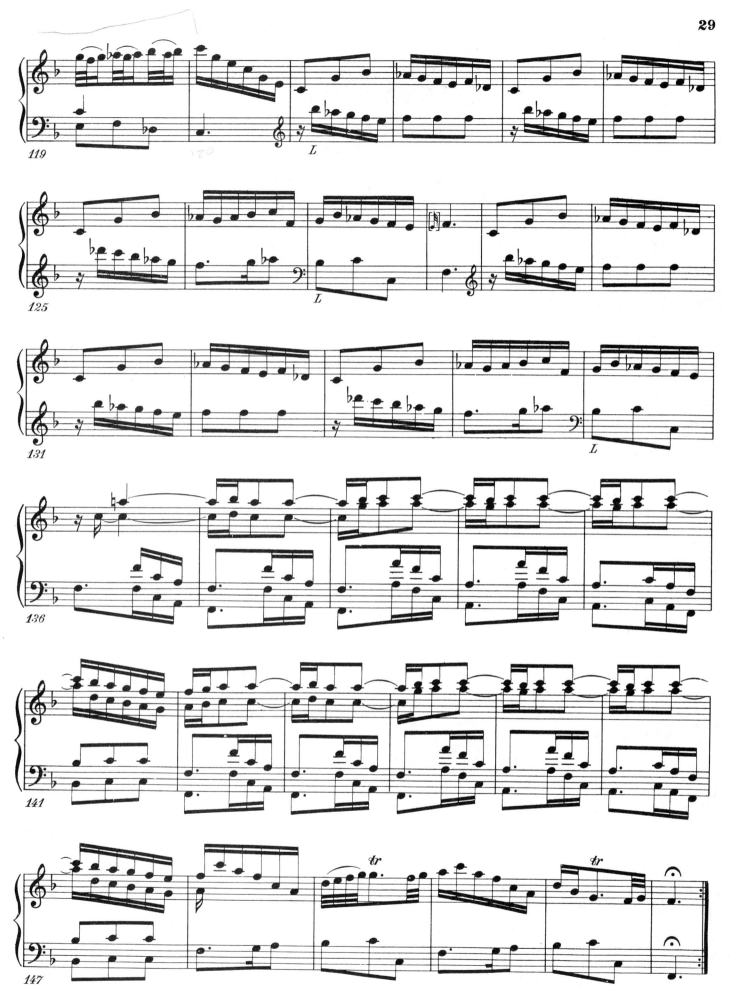

K. 46
Venice XIV 4, Parma II 15, Worgan 34
Longo 25

39

46

53

59

65

71

111

117

123

128

133

139

K. 54
Venice XIV 12, Parma III 20, Worgan 12
Longo 241

36

42916

K. 57
Venice XIV 15, Parma III 12, Worgan 20
Longo S. 38

96

104

113

120

127

134

K. 84
Venice XIV 49
Longo 10

XI

K. 52
Venice XIV 10 and 61
Longo 267

Andante moderato

XII

5

10

15

20

25

46

K. 96
Venice XV 6, Parma III 29, Worgan 33
Longo 465

Allegrissimo

42916

48

42916

K. 105
Venice XV 8, Parma III 24, Worgan 36
Longo 204

XIV

Allegro

46

55

63

70

78

86

137

144

151

158

165

172

54

K. 115
Venice XV 18, Parma III 13, Worgan 23
Longo 407

Allegro

XV

6

11

16

21

25

42916

56

42916

81

85

89

94

100

104

K. 116
Venice XV 19, Parma III 14 Worgan 24
Longo 452

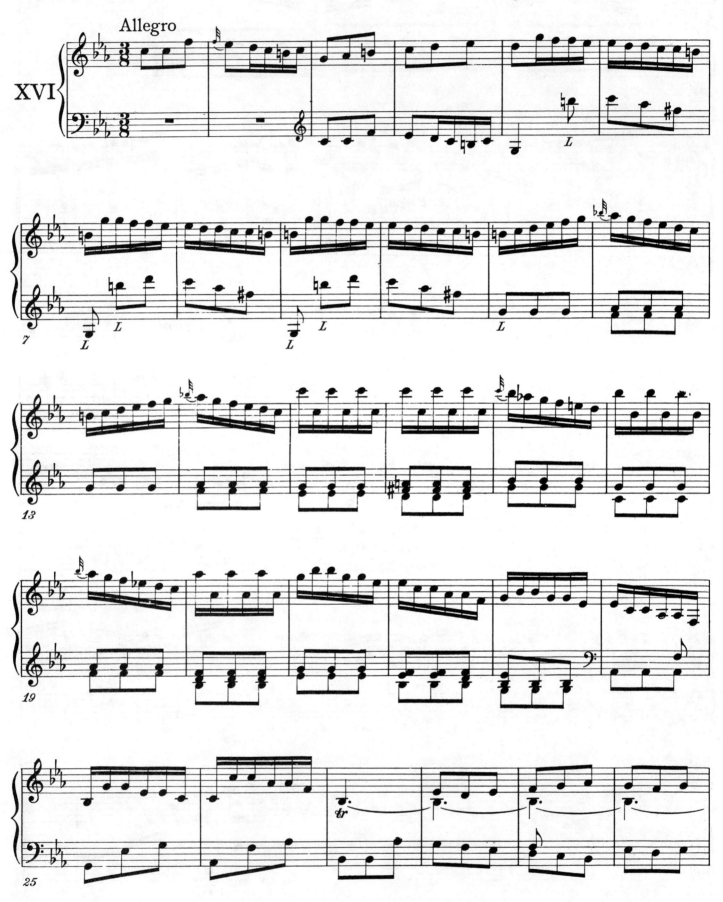

62

K. 119
Venice XV 22, Parma II 17, Worgan 39
Longo 415

42916

Tremulo nell' A la mi re

64

96

106

116

126

135

144

42916

154

163

172

181

190

199

66

K. 120
Venice XV 23, Parma II 16, Worgan 28
Longo 215

XVIII

Allegrissimo

K. 132
Venice XV 35, Parma V 5
Longo 457

42916

39

43

47

51

55

74

K. 133
Venice XV 36, Parma V 6
Longo 282

Allegro

XX

8

15

22

29

42916

71

79

87

95

103

78

K. 175
Venice I 28, Parma I 28
Longo 429

Allegro

XXK

5

10

15

21

42916

82

K. 140
Venice II 16, Parma III 25, Worgan 37
Longo 107

Allegro

XXII

4

9

13

16

20

42916

K. 208
Venice III 3, Parma IV 1
Longo 238

42916

86

K. 209
Venice III 4, Parma IV 2
Longo 428

K. 215
Venice III 10, Parma IV 25
Longo 323

Andante

XXV

42916

67

72

77

81

85

K. 216
Venice III 11, Parma IV 26
Longo 273

Allegro

XXVI

6

12

18

24

30

36

41

46

50

55

62

96

42916

K. 238
Venice IV 3, Parma V 21
Longo 27

XXVII

K. 239
Venice IV 4, Parma V 22
Longo 281

Allegro

XXVIII

18

23

28

32

35

38

42

46

50

54

K. 259
Venice IV 24, Parma VI 15
Longo 103

K. 260
Venice IV 25, Parma VI 16
Longo 124

Allegro

XXX

110

97

107

116

125

134

143

42916

152

160

168

177

186

195